A MANUAL FOR HEARING GOD AND GIVIN

GOD IS
SPEAKING
CAN YOU HEAR HIM?

JOSEPH GIL

Cover design by Christian Wetzel

Published by:
Coast Christian Fellowship
4000 Pacific Coast Highway
Torrance, CA 90505
www.coastchristian.org

Table of Contents:

PART 1 - GOD IS SPEAKING

Introduction - Pg. 6
1. All Can Hear - Pg. 8
2. A New Operating System - Pg. 10
3. The Unseen Realm - Pg. 12
4. Distinguishing His Voice - Pg. 15
5. By Faith - Pg. 18
6. The Ways God Communicates - Pg. 20
7. Valuing His Presence - Pg. 23

PART 2 - THE GIFT OF PROPHECY

Introduction - Pg. 29
1. The Gift of Prophecy - Pg. 30
2. The Purpose of Prophecy - Pg. 32
3. The Heart of Prophecy - Pg. 34
4. New Testament Prophecy - Pg. 35
5. The Power of Prophecy - Pg. 38

PART 3 - A HEALTHY PROPHETIC COMMUNITY

Introduction - Pg. 44
1. False Prophets - Pg. 45
2. Judging Prophetic Words - Pg. 46
3. Seeing People the Way God Sees them - Pg. 47
4. Functioning with the Rest of the Body - Pg. 48
5. Identity Before Gifting - Pg. 49
6. Core Beliefs - Pg. 50
7. Changing Your World - Pg. 51

NOTES

PART 1
GOD IS SPEAKING

PART 1
GOD IS SPEAKING

INTRODUCTION

I started getting to know God when I was 19 years old. I read the Bible everyday starting from the first page. The first story that really caught my attention was about Moses who talked with God face to face. That story set the standard for my relationship with God. I did not grow up in church so I knew nothing else about God but what I read in the Bible. I read that it was possible to talk to God face to face! He actually met with a man and had a two-way conversation. That was all I needed to know. So without much effort or reverence I talked with God in those early years as if He was sitting next to me on my bed. I talked with Him in the car, in class, while waiting in line at the mall. I would tell Him about the pizza I ate and the cars I liked. I would ask Him things that confused me and would get answers back that brought clarity. It was an amazing relationship until I heard a Bible scholar teach that it wasn't possible, that God only speaks through the Bible and anything beyond that was dangerous. The last thing I wanted to do was something that could jeopardize my devotion to God. So my conversations stopped

for a while and I was downgraded to talking about God instead of talking with Him. I still prayed but didn't expect a response. It became more of a formality than anything else.

> *Through those stories God reveals how He relates to His people and they become an invitation to more.*

But, I am so thankful that God continued to speak to me. I had dreams that revealed what God was about to do and came true. I would get inklings of what people were going through and when I called them, it was a 'coincidence' or 'perfect timing.' Eventually I began to trust again that my conversations with God were real. It was true that God does speak to us through the Bible but He does not want it to stop there. Through those stories God reveals how He relates to His people and they become an invitation to more. An enticing invitation to communicate to God as Moses, Abraham and Isaiah did!

6

Face to face, as a friend talks to a friend. This has been my pursuit, to know Him and to help others know Him closer than before.

There are some elementary principles in this life that we all would agree on. One of them is obeying God. All of us want to please the One in whom we have our origin. How do we accomplish this? There are some who still believe that God only speaks through the Bible. For them I guess this class is of no use. Of course the Bible is God's number one source of making Himself known. The Bible is also the final say on every matter without a doubt. We have the Bible as our owners manual and our compass in an always changing world. In this we will never deviate. However, we may hold the Bible in the highest regards and still miss the point of it. It exists to show us what's possible! Each example in the Bible provokes me to a healthy jealousy. I am not satisfied with reading about Moses talking with God face to face without experiencing it myself. I do not find satisfaction in hearing about Enoch walking with God if I am denied the same lifestyle. It would be useless to read about how the Lord spoke to Joseph through dreams and never ask God to speak to us in the same way. It says in Deuteronomy, "He humbled you and let you be hungry, and fed you with manna which you did not know, nor did your fathers know, that He might make you understand that man does not live by bread alone, but man lives by everything that proceeds out of the mouth of the Lord" *(Deuteronomy 8:3)*.

> *We may hold the Bible in the highest regards and still miss the point of it. It exists to show us what's possible!*

I have always been thrilled with the prospect of hearing from God personally and directly. I have realized over the years that when God speaks to me, I come alive. I have become addicted and dependent on the voice of my Father. It matters less and less to me the content of the message these days. It's His very presence that I am eternally attracted to. To be able to communicate with the God of the universe is a privilege beyond comparison.

I realize that isn't everyone'sexperience. That is the reason for this class. Hopefully somehow, God will use the words on these pages to open the door of communicating with the One and only true God.

1. The Spirit was Poured Out on All so All Can Hear

Hearing God's voice is central to the Gospel message. Jesus preached that the 'Kingdom of God is here.' He said all you need is eyes to see and ears to hear. In the Old Testament only a few had the ability to hear the Spirit. God was selective and the Spirit did not rest on the masses. However, there was a prophecy in Joel that promised one day the Spirit would be poured out on everyone!

> *"It will come about after this*
> *That I will pour out My Spirit on all mankind;*
> *And your sons and daughters will prophesy,*
> *Your old men will dream dreams,*
> *Your young men will see visions.*
> *Even on the male and female servants*
> *I will pour out My Spirit in those days."*
> *(Joel 2:28-29)*

In your own words, what did God promise His people in the book of Joel?

Pour out His spirit

Who did this apply to?

ALL WHO BELIEVE

This was a great promise. To the people who heard these words it was an out of the box concept. It meant that everyone, young and old, no matter their economic status or their gender, would be filled with the Spirit of God and God would speak to them. This was a privilege that was respected and desired by all that loved God.

> *It meant that everyone, young and old, no matter their economic status or their gender, would be filled with the Spirit of God and God would speak to them.*

The promise we read in Joel came to pass in Acts chapter 2 with those waiting on God in the Upper Room:

> *But Peter, taking his stand with the eleven, raised his voice and declared*
> *to them: "Men of Judea and all you who live in Jerusalem, let this be known*
> *to you and give heed to my words. For these men are not drunk, as you*
> *suppose, for it is only the third hour of the day; but this is what was spoken*
> *of through the prophet Joel:*
> *"And it shall be in the last days,' God says,*

'That I will pour forth of MY Spirit on all mankind;
And your sons and your daughters shall prophesy,
And your young men shall see visions,
And your old men shall dream dreams;
Even on MY bondslaves, both men and women,
I will in those days pour forth of MY Spirit
And they shall prophesy."
(Acts 2:14-18)

What is available to you according to these verses in Acts?

Baptism of Holy Spirit

We are living on the other side of this promise. In fact, it is no longer in the 'promise' category because it is now a reality and can be accessed by all.

- The Spirit has been poured out on ___US___ .
- The Spirit enables a person to ___Communicate___ with God.
- It is the same Spirit that enabled people to ___Prophecy___ in the Old Tesament.

No longer do I call you slaves, for the slave does not know what his master is
doing; but I have called you friends, for all things that I have heard from My
Father I have made known to you. (John 15:15)

2. Hearing God Takes a New Operating System

One of the greatest goals in my life and the reason for this class is to connect people to our loving Father. Unfortunately my experience has been that a good percentage of Christians are not experiencing a two-way relationship with God. I have noticed a major pattern that hinders God's people from hearing His voice, it is found in our perception of God as a good Father. Your early stages of development contribute to how you view your heavenly Father today. If you seldom experienced the distinct pleasure of a proud earthly dad as he observed your life, you may not be experiencing the true Papa God.

Describe your own experience with your father growing up:

_____

_____

_____

_____

_____

Ask the Holy Spirit how this has affected your relationship with God:

_____

_____

_____

_____

"This is My beloved Son, in whom I am well-pleased"
(Matthew 3:17).

Jesus felt the pleasure of His Father throughout His entire life except for one moment. When Jesus became sin on the cross His Father looked away and was not pleased. This I believe was the most agonizing torment in Jesus' entire earthly experience. He cried out a statement that could sum up something we have all felt at one time or another,

"MY God, MY God, why have You forsaken ME?" (Matthew 27:46).

The good news is that He became sin for us so that we would not have to experience separation from God. We have been given the Spirit of adoption as children of God so that we now can experience the pleasure of the Father just as Jesus does. Now that is truly amazing!

> *The good news is that He became sin for us so that we would not have to experience separation from God.*

How does God feel about you?

He loves me enough to send his Son to die for my sins and no longer imputes my sins to me

gave me Christ spirit and mind, and faith

Our concept of God dramatically influences our level of hearing His voice.

For you have not received a spirit of slavery leading to fear again, but you have received a spirit of adoption as sons by which we cry out, "Abba! Father!"
(Romans 8:15)

No longer do I call you slaves, for the slave does not know what his master is doing; but I have called you friends, for all things that I have heard from My Father I have made known to you. (John 15:15)

Who are you according to these verses?

an adopted son of God joint heir with Christ

- My position in God has forever been _established_ by the death and resurrection of Jesus.

- I have been _adopted_ into the royal family and God is my Papa.

- My ability to communicate with God is _____ and He is always _listening_.

Based on these truths, what do you expect from God today?

_____

_____

_____

We are destroying speculations and every lofty thing raised up
against the knowledge of God, and we are taking every thought
captive to the obedience of Christ, (2 Corinthians 10:5)

But you are a chosen race, a royal priesthood, a holy nation, a people for God's own
possession, so that you may proclaim the excellencies of Him who has called you out of
darkness into His marvelous light; for you once were not A people, but now you are the
people of God; you had not received mercy, but now you have received mercy.
(1 Peter 2:9-10)

3. The Unseen Realm - A New Way of 'Seeing' and 'Hearing'

There is another world that exists that cannot be seen by the natural eye. It is present and active right now, all around us. Jesus was aware of this realm and referenced it often when He spoke of the 'kingdom.' The throne room of God that the Apostle John saw in the book of Revelation is a present reality and glimpse into the spirit realm. God does not want us to be ignorant of these things. We are spirit beings and were built to be able to function in this other world. The difficult part is practicing your spirit 'muscle' to get used to seeing with your spiritual eyes instead of your natural eyes. (Eyes is used here metaphorically.)

But a natural man does not accept the things of the Spirit of God, for they are foolishness to him; and he cannot understand them, because they are spiritually appraised. But he who is spiritual appraises all things, yet he himself is appraised by no one. For who has known the mind of the Lord, that he will instruct Him? But we have the mind of Christ. (1 Corinthians 2:14-16)

Explain this verse below in your own words:

From that time Jesus began to preach and say, " Repent, for the kingdom of heaven is at hand." (Matthew 4:17)

_____

_____

_____

Repent means to change the way you think. Adopting a new belief system about the nearness of God is imperative to hearing His voice on a consistent basis. If you don't believe He is near, you won't be able to hear.

In order to communicate with God we must know something about His nature. He is first a spirit being, He calls His followers to worship Him according to His nature, not ours. *"God is spirit, and those who worship Him must worship in spirit and truth" (John 4:24).* Spirit refers to the invisible world beyond the physical. Truth is that which corresponds with reality, which is according to the Biblical foundation of who He is and how He has instructed us to approach Him. Being brought up with a Western perspective, we often have a difficult time with things that are invisible. However, you were designed to thrive in His environment!

Now concerning spiritual gifts, brethren, I do not want you to be unaware.
(1 Corinthians 12:1)

In the original text the word 'gifts' is not present. It would be more precise to read, "Concerning the spiritual..." He is referring to a concept that encompasses God's native world and things that are invisible to our natural eyes. The next thing Paul says about this invisible world is that he does not want them to be "unaware." This is the same word as 'ignorant' or 'unconscious of.'

Spiritual:

_____

Opposite of unaware:

_____

The unseen realm is not an unfamiliar concept. When someone pulls out a gun in a public place, everyone can 'feel' the fear in the air. When you know two family members are at odds at a party, you can 'sense' the tension. All of these tangible elements in our world like love and hate are real even though invisible. They may be difficult to describe their substance but everyone acknowledges their existence.

- There exists an _____ realm that I am a part of.

- God is _____ and I am built to engage Him in spirit.

- Now that I am born again, I am _____ and can _____ in the invisible world.

Example: Two Coexisting Realms

Then another sign appeared in heaven: and behold, a great red dragon having seven heads and ten horns, and on his heads were seven diadems. And his tail *swept away a third of the stars of heaven and threw them to the earth. And the dragon stood before the woman who was about to give birth, so that when she gave birth he might devour her child.
(Revelation 12:3-4)

_____

_____

_____

_____

Then when Herod saw that he had been tricked by the magi, he became very enraged, and sent and slew all the male children who were in Bethlehem and all its vicinity, from two years old and under, according to the time which he had determined from the magi. (Matthew 2:16)

_____

_____

_____

Which realm is superior and why?

_____

_____

_____

_____

4. Distinguishing His Voice from Other Voices

One of the most difficult things in hearing the voice of God is that there are other voices competing for your attention. Most people will listen to the voice that is most familiar. This familiarity is developed in your early years growing up. The words and tone of voice your parents or guardians used toward you became your norm. This can be a help or a hinderance in hearing God's voice. Some readily accept the words of the accuser who condemns even if their 'theology' tells them otherwise. Why is this? There is a difference in believing the Bible with your intellect and believing the Bible in your heart. You can believe it to be true in a vacuum but when life's pressures are squeezing in on you, the core beliefs of the heart come to the surface. In these times instead of falling into discouragement, we take note of those other voices so that we can eventually recognize them and overcome them.

WE USUALLY HEAR ONE OF FOUR VOICES:

God

_____

_____

Ourselves

_____

_____

The World

_____

_____

The Enemy

_____

_____

What does He sound like to you?

_____

_____

_____

_____

The Spirit of God has a feeling, a set of beliefs, an attitude, and a motivation.

> _And the tempter came and said to Him, "If You are the Son of God,_
> _command that these stones become bread." (Matthew 4:3)_

- The enemy's voice causes you to have to _____ yourself.

- Your spirit desires good things but must still be _____ from God's Spirit.

- God's voice already _____ in you and tells you who you already are!

- We must examine the _____ by _____ ourselves with the Spirit of God.

> _Beloved, do not believe every spirit, but test the spirits to see whether they are_
> _from God, because many false prophets have gone out into the world._
> _(1 John 4:1)_

KNOWING GOD'S HEART

Over the years God's heart has been misunderstood by millions of people. God has been blamed for terrible tragedies over the course of history. When we read about His actions, we tend to determine His motives based on our understanding. When we read stories like Job, Ananias and Saphira, and God destroying cities, we have to ask Him what His heart was behind those actions without assuming God's motivations.

In the Old Testament we see entire towns destroyed by the direction of God to Israel. We have to be careful or we might misinterpret His heart behind these actions. His heart was always to bless the entire population. His goal was and still is to cover the earth with His glory. He wanted them to repent and be blessed. His war was never against people but against principalities and false gods who were destroying humanity. When light comes into a region, darkness has to flee. If people are attached to darkness more than to God, they will have to go as well. There's no other option. If Goliath would have repented, his head would not have been cut off. Nineveh was one city that did repent and God blessed them instead of destroying them. Think of Jesus who washed Judas' feet knowing full well that he was going to backstab Him. It is in these revelations that we begin to understand the heart of God. This is extremely important because when we understand the heart of God then we will correctly recognize His voice.

> *Think of Jesus who washed Judas' feet knowing full well that he was going to backstab Him. It is in these revelations that we begin to understand the heart of God.*

• God desires to _____ the human race.

• All humans were made in the _____ of God and to be _____ of God.

• When God intervenes on earth, His motivation is _____.

For while we were still helpless, at the right time Christ died for the ungodly. For one will hardly die for a righteous man; though perhaps for the good man someone would dare even to die. But God demonstrates His own love toward us, in that while we were yet sinners, Christ died for us. Much more then, having now been justified by His blood, we shall be saved from the wrath of God through Him. For if while we were enemies we were reconciled to God through the death of His Son, much more, having been reconciled, we shall be saved by His life. (Romans 5:6-10)

What is God's heart toward you?

_____

_____

_____

_____

_____

_____

5. We Enter this Relationship with God by Faith

Now faith is the assurance of things hoped for, the conviction of things not seen.
For by it the men of old gained approval. (Hebrews 11:1-2)

You may have heard these concepts before. Whether you are an experienced Bible scholar or are hearing for the first time, in order for these truths to take effect in your life, you must receive them by faith. There is a saying, "I'll believe it when I see it." This is backwards from the way the kingdom works. In the kingdom when you believe it, you will begin to 'see' it. We never want to adopt an attitude that expects God to prove Himself to us. **God doesn't move towards pity parties, He moves toward confident faith!**

Let's declare some undeniable facts so that they can become a reality for us. Take time to ponder each one and allow your heart to receive them. Commit them into your belief system.

- When Jesus died, the veil of the Holy of Holies was torn in two, signifying that the barrier to intimacy with God between Him and I was removed.

- Jesus said that He would be with me always, and that He would never leave me.

- The Holy Spirit who is God has taken up residence inside of me permanently, which makes me a walking temple of God. I am a host of His presence.

- I have been elevated to a child of God, I am now able to hear my Father's voice as Jesus did.

- Because of Jesus' death on the cross, there is no barrier between God and I.

If there are any thoughts or feelings that contradict any of these declarations, you will have to choose which is truth and which is a lie. Let me give you a hint... the Bible is always right. ☺

Why did the original Israelites not get to enter into the Promised Land?

_____

_____

_____

_____

_____

_____

• So we see that they were not able to enter because of _____.
  (Hebrews 3:19)

• Unbelief is a sin that keeps people from entering into the _____ of God.

• For what does the Scripture say? " Abraham _____ God, and it was
  credited to him as righteousness." *(Romans 4:3)*

We enter into this victorious life by faith. We choose to believe what God says about us
and what was accomplished on the cross. We believe that we have the same Spirit that
Jesus had when He walked the earth. We believe that we are co-heirs, we have been
elevated to the status of Jesus in relation to the Father.

*And without faith it is impossible to please Him, for he who comes to God must believe
that He is and that He is a rewarder of those who seek Him. (Hebrews 11:6)*

_____

_____

6. The Ways God Communicates

It is the glory of God to conceal a matter, but the glory of kings is to search out a matter.
(Proverbs 25:2)

Wouldn't it be nice if God gave us a printed itinerary for the next five years of our lives? It seems like it would be much easier if we were clear about what He has planned ahead of time. So why then does God speak in riddles? First, we must look at God's priorities. We have to remember that God is more concerned with us knowing Him intimately rather than being in a particular place or doing a particular thing. If His main priority is that we live in a certain city and have a certain job, then He would most definitely make that clear to us. However, His main priority is relationship, so He designed a plan for our lives that promotes relationship before anything else. Therefore a printed itinerary might be clear but it has the potential to cause us to be independent of the One who is directing us. God would not give us anything that would jeopardize our relationship with Him. Isn't He good?

> *His main priority is relationship, so He designed a plan for our*
> *lives that promotes relationship before anything else.*

- God is interested in _____ with us more than He is concerned with us 'getting it right.'

*Now Moses was pasturing the flock of Jethro his father-in-law, the priest of Midian; and he led the flock to the west side of the wilderness and came to Horeb, the mountain of God. The angel of the Lord appeared to him in a blazing fire from the midst of a bush; and he looked, and behold, the bush was burning with fire, yet the bush was not consumed. So Moses said, " I must **turn aside** now and see this marvelous sight, why the bush is not burned up." When the Lord saw that he **turned aside** to look, God called to him from the midst of the bush and said, "Moses, Moses!" And he said, "Here I am." (Exodus 3:1-4 Emphasis Added)*

What does 'turning aside' look like in your life?

_____

_____

_____

• God is deliberately vague to encourage us to _____.

> *And the disciples came and said to Him, "Why do You speak to them in parables?" Jesus answered them, "To you it has been granted to know the mysteries of the kingdom of heaven, but to them it has not been granted." (Matthew 13:10-11)*

> *At that time Jesus said, "I praise You, Father, Lord of heaven and earth, that You have hidden these things from the wise and intelligent and have revealed them to infants." (Matthew 11:25)*

Three Parts to Hearing God

1. Revelation

_____

_____

2. Interpretation

_____

_____

3. Application

_____

_____

Follow up questions for the Spirit:

• What does this mean?
• Is this for me or for someone else?
• Is this for now or for a future time?
• When do you want me to share it?
• What do you want me to do with this?
• If unsure, ask a leader.

WAYS GOD HAS SPOKEN IN THE BIBLE

Internal Voice

_____

_____

Audible Voice of God

_____

_____

Vision

_____

_____

Dream

_____

_____

Trance

_____

_____

Angelic Visitation

_____

_____

Signs and Wonders

_____

_____

Burdens

_____

_____

The Revelation of Jesus Christ, which God gave Him to show to His bond-servants, the things which must soon take place; and He sent and communicated it by His angel to His bond-servant John, who testified to the word of God and to the testimony of Jesus Christ, even to all that he saw. (Revelation 1:1-2)

Path of communication of a prophetic revelation:

---

7. Valuing His Presence

What is your most valuable possession? What will you protect with your life? Whatever you treasure the most will greatly influence your choices. Many people want to hear God but do not take the time to wait for Him. His words may not be as valuable as other things on a given day. Others value His voice so much that they will wait for Him for days on end like they did before the great outpouring on Azuza Street in 1906. Those that choose to value the presence of God will guard their time with Him. When He begins to speak they will stop whatever they are doing to yield to that One Voice. Those that truly value the presence of God will hear His voice on a continual basis.

Those that truly value the presence of God will hear His voice on a continual basis.

It was at this time that He went off to the mountain to pray, and He spent the whole night in prayer to God. And when day came, He called His disciples to Him and chose twelve of them, whom He also named as apostles: (Luke 6:12-13)

The Process of Quieting Yourself

_____

_____

Surrender your Future

_____

_____

Come to Him without an Agenda

_____

_____

Come with a Yes in Your Spirit

_____

_____

- I purposefully seek the Lord on a regular basis to _____ with Him.

- I spend time seeking what's on _____ heart.

- Hosting His presence is not an event but a _____.

And do not get drunk with wine, for that is dissipation, but be filled with the Spirit, speaking to one another in psalms and hymns and spiritual songs, singing and making melody with your heart to the Lord; always giving thanks for all things in the name of our Lord Jesus Christ to God, even the Father; and be subject to one another in the fear of Christ. (Ephesians 5:18-21)

One thing I have asked from the Lord, that I shall seek: That I may dwell in the house of the Lord all the days of my life, To behold the beauty of the Lord and to meditate in His temple. (Psalms 27:4)

PART 2
THE GIFT OF PROPHECY

PART 2
THE GIFT OF PROPHECY

INTRODUCTION

The next step to hearing God is to hear God for others. If hearing God is one of our greatest assets then we naturally want others to benefit from our treasure. Receiving a message from God for someone else is called prophecy. Part two of this class introduces this gift. We are going to take all the principles we learned about hearing God and apply it to hearing God for others; this is called prophecy.

> *'And it shall be in the last days,' God says,*
> *'That I will pour forth of MY Spirit on all mankind;*
> *And your sons and your daughters shall prophesy,*
> *And your young men shall see visions,*
> *And your old men shall dream dreams;*
> *Even on MY bondslaves, both men and women,*
> *I will in those days pour forth of MY Spirit*
> *And they shall prophesy.'*
> *(Acts 2:17-18)*

Dreams and visions were ways that God revealed His message to the Prophets of the Old Testament. God has released that to "all flesh" or everyone, mankind. Everyone now has access to prophecy through the Holy Spirit. This is extremely valuable because God wants to communicate to His people and you are the instrument He wants to use. When God says, "I love you" to one of His own, He often uses another person.

> *But Moses said to him, "Are you jealous for my sake? Would that all the Lord's people were prophets, that the Lord would put His Spirit upon them!"*
> *(Numbers 11:29)*

This is extremely valuable because God wants to communicate to His people and you are the instrument He wants to use.

1. The Gift of Prophecy

Prophecy is one of the gifts that the Holy Spirit distributes to the Body of Christ. The gift of prophecy is a supernatural power that enables people to perceive and speak the very heart and mind of the Lord. Prophecy is the declaration of that which cannot be known by natural means, it is the forth-telling of the will of God, whether with reference to the past, the present, or the future. The gift is not a reward for good behavior but it is free to those who seek it. Within the gifts of the New Testament mentioned by Paul, prophecy is the gift most esteemed and deemed the most valuable for building up the church *(1 Corinthians 14:1-5)*. The gift is ultimately to bring God and His people closer together.

An Example of Prophecy – The Book of Revelation
"The Revealing of Jesus Christ"

> *The Revelation of Jesus Christ, which God gave Him to show to His bond-servants, the things which must soon take place; and He sent and communicated it by His angel to His bond-servant John, who testified to the word of God and to the testimony of Jesus Christ, even to all that he saw. Blessed is he who reads and those who hear the words of the prophecy, and heed the things which are written in it; for the time is near.*
> *(Revelation 1:1-3)*

• This prophecy was given in the heart of _____. So that we might know

what the _____ is doing.

> *No longer do I call you slaves, for the slave does not know what his master is doing; but I have called you friends, for all things that I have heard from My Father I have made known to you. (John 15:15)*

CHAIN OF COMMUNICATION

Given by the Father to Jesus ► From Jesus to an angel ► From an angel to John ► From John to the messenger of the seven churches ► from the messenger to the congregation.

• John received it by being _____.

I was in the Spirit on the Lord's Day, and I heard behind me a loud
voice like the sound of a trumpet, (Revelation 1:10)

• John was asked to _____ it down and _____ it to the churches.

• John was not told to _____ it or explain how to _____ it.

"Write in a book what you see, and send it to the seven churches"
(Revelation 1:11)

• We are told to _____ it and _____ it.

Blessed is he who reads and those who hear the words of the prophecy,
and heed the things which are written in it; for the time is near.
(Revelation 1:3)

HOW DO YOU GET PROPHECY?

Pursue love, yet desire earnestly spiritual gifts, but especially
that you may prophesy. (1 Corinthians 14:1)

"If you then, being evil, know how to give good gifts to your children, how much more
will your heavenly Father give the Holy Spirit to those who ask Him?"
(Luke 11:13)

• You receive the gift of prophecy by _____, you receive prophecy

by _____.

Asking and Risking

_____

_____

_____

Waiting on the Movement of the Holy Spirit

_____

_____

_____

2. The Purpose of Prophecy

Spirit of Elijah

> *"Behold, I am going to send you Elijah the prophet before the coming of the great and terrible day of the Lord. He will restore the hearts of the fathers to their children and the hearts of the children to their fathers, so that I will not come and smite the land with a curse. (Malachi 4:5-6)*

What was Elijah known for? Breaking up domestic fights between fathers and sons? No, he reconciled the children of Israel to their Father when he proved that the prophets of Baal were powerless and that Yahweh was the true God. This is what the next prophet was going to do.

Next we have John the Baptist on the scene. Jesus said about him:

> *For all the prophets and the Law prophesied until John. And if you are willing to accept it, John himself is Elijah who was to come. He who has ears to hear, let him hear. (Matthew 11:13-15)*

What John did interprets the passage in Malachi. He called the people of Israel back to God. He said repent by changing the orientation of your heart. He restored the hearts of the children back to their Father.

• The overarching job of the prophet, and the primary function of prophecy is to

_____ the _____ of the children back to the Father.

_____

_____

_____

Pursue love, yet desire earnestly spiritual gifts, but especially that you may prophesy. For one who speaks in a tongue does not speak to men but to God; for no one understands, but in his spirit he speaks mysteries. But one who prophesies speaks to men for edification and exhortation and consolation. One who speaks in a tongue edifies himself; but one who prophesies edifies the church. Now I wish that you all spoke in tongues, but even more that you would prophesy; and greater is one who prophesies than one who speaks in tongues, unless he interprets, so that the church may receive edifying.
(1 Corinthians 14:1-5)

* Key Verse for New Testament Prophecy

But one who prophesies speaks to men for edification and exhortation and consolation.
(1 Corinthians 14:3)

Edification - "To _____ a house"

Edification is to encourage someone to the point of a permanent transformation in the way they see themselves. Calling them to account of the high call of Jesus on their life.

But you are a chosen race, a royal priesthood, a holy nation, a people for God's own possession, so that you may proclaim the excellencies of Him who has called you out of darkness into His marvelous light; for you once were not a people, but now you are the people of God; you had not received mercy, but now you have received mercy. Beloved, I urge you as aliens and strangers to abstain from fleshly lusts, which wage war against the soul.
(1 Peter 2:9-11)

> *Edification is to encourage someone to the point of a permanent transformation in the way they see themselves. Calling them to account of the high call of Jesus on their life.*

Exhortation - "A calling to come _____"

Exhortation is to reconcile a person to God in every aspect of their life.

Now all these things are from God, who reconciled us to Himself through Christ and gave us the ministry of reconciliation, (2 Corinthians 5:18)

Consolation - "Speaking _____"

Consolation is a tender, soothing communication that results in the comfort of the individual.

Since you have in obedience to the truth purified your souls for a sincere love of the brethren, fervently love one another from the heart, (1 Peter 1:22)

The ABCD's of prophecy - For Kids

• Always _____, _____, _____

_____

_____

_____

*But one who prophesies speaks to men for edification and
exhortation and consolation. (1 Corinthians 14:3)*

3. The Heart of Prophecy

At the heart of the gift of prophecy is the motivation to love and serve those you are prophesying to. If prophecy is 'speaking on behalf of God,' then the motivation of prophecy should match the heart of God as do the words match what He is saying. God is in love with His Bride the Church and wants to communicate to her. When He does, He wants the message to be brought forth with tenderness and care. To misrepresent God's heart is just as detrimental as giving a false prophetic word. You can have the right word but the wrong spirit behind it. Misrepresenting God's heart has the potential to cause a lot of damage, especially if the person is in a position of authority. Prophecy without love amounts to nothing.

*If I speak with the tongues of men and of angels, but do not have love, I have
become a noisy gong or a clanging cymbal. If I have the gift of prophecy, and
know all mysteries and all knowledge; and if I have all faith, so as to remove
mountains, but do not have love, I am nothing. (1 Corinthians 13:1-2)*

Replace love with the gift of prophecy:

_____ is patient,

_____ is kind and is not jealous;

_____ does not brag and is not arrogant, does not act unbecomingly; it does not seek its own, is not provoked, does not take into account a wrong suffered, does not rejoice in unrighteousness, but rejoices with the truth; bears all things, believes all things, hopes all things, endures all things.

_____ never fails. *(1 Corinthians 13:4-8)*

"Not everyone who says to Me, 'Lord, Lord,' will enter the kingdom of heaven, but he who does the will of My Father who is in heaven will enter. Many will say to Me on that day, 'Lord, Lord, did we not prophesy in Your name, and in Your name cast out demons, and in Your name perform many miracles?' And then I will declare to them, 'I never knew you; depart from ME, you who practice lawlessness.' (Matthew 7:21-2)

What does 'in the name of Jesus' mean?

_____

_____

_____

_____

4. New Covenant Prophecy

The prophet's job under the old covenant was to judge according to the law. When Jesus died and rose from the dead we entered a new covenant. The prophet's job under the new covenant is to reconcile the world to God. Some are still operating under the old covenant and treating people as though God requires payment for sin. The death of Jesus paid for sin and conquered death. This new covenant has a new set of rules and expectations for the believer, as well as benefits.

> *When Jesus died and rose from the dead we entered a new covenant. The prophet's job under the new covenant is to reconcile the world to God.*

"The Law and the Prophets were proclaimed until John; since that time the gospel of the kingdom of God has been preached, and everyone is forcing his way into it." (Luke 16:16)

But now He has obtained a more excellent ministry, by as much as He is also the mediator of a better covenant, which has been enacted on better promises. For if that first covenant had been faultless, there would have been no occasion sought for a second. For finding fault with them, He says,

"Behold, days are coming, says the Lord, When I will effect a new covenant
With the house of Israel and with the house of Judah;
Not like the covenant which I made with their fathers on the day when I took them by the hand to lead them out of the land of Egypt;
For they did not continue in MY covenant,
And I did not care for them, says the Lord.
"For this is the covenant that I will make with the house of Israel
After those days, says the Lord: I will put MY laws into their minds,
And I will write them on their hearts. And I will be their God,
And they shall be MY people.
"And they shall not teach everyone his fellow citizen,
And everyone his brother, saying, 'Know the Lord,' For all will know ME,
From the least to the greatest of them.
"For I will be merciful to their iniquities, And I will remember their sins no more."
When He said, " A new covenant," He has made the first obsolete.
But whatever is becoming obsolete and growing old is ready to disappear.
(Hebrews 8:6-13)

But He turned and rebuked them, and said, "You do not know what kind of spirit you are of; for the Son of Man did not come to destroy men's lives, but to save them. (Luke 9:55-56)

Therefore, my brethren, you also were made to die to the Law through the body of Christ, so that you might be joined to another, to Him who was raised from the dead, in order that we might bear fruit for God. (Romans 7:4)

Old Covenant

- Breaking the Law deserved _____.

- The prophets were the ones who _____ the Law.

- Death was the penalty for _____.

- Whole cities were _____ because of sin.

- Sinners were unclean and to be _____ at all costs.

- The message of prophecy was to get right or _____ the consequences.

New Covenant

- The penalty of sin was _____ in full.

- The prophets proclaim the good news of _____.

- Death and the grave were _____ by love.

- Whole cities are being _____ because of His blood.

- Sinners are to be _____ because we have the antidote to sin.

- The message of prophecy is focused on _____ because of the redemptive work of the cross and the filling of the Holy Spirit.

Therefore from now on we recognize no one according to the flesh; even though we have known Christ according to the flesh, yet now we know Him in this way no longer. Therefore if anyone is in Christ, he is a new creature; the old things passed away; behold, new things have come. Now all these things are from God, who reconciled us to Himself through Christ and gave us the ministry of reconciliation, namely, that God was in Christ reconciling the world to Himself, not counting their trespasses against them, and He has committed to us the word of reconciliation. Therefore, we are ambassadors for Christ, as though God were making an appeal through us; we beg you on behalf of Christ, be reconciled to God. He made Him who knew no sin to be sin on our behalf, so that we might become the righteousness of God in Him. (2 Corinthians 5:16-21)

5. The Power of Prophecy

Prophecy is God's thoughts spoken into the atmosphere. The spoken word of God is one of the most powerful tools we possess. We see this power at work in Genesis chapter one when God spoke the universe into existence. **His words created worlds!** This supernatural power changes circumstances, atmospheres and history. A spoken word from God cannot be underestimated. Prophecy is not just a cool sign. The prophetic has the potential to change the course of history, and propel you into your destiny.

Then God said, "Let there be light"; and there was light.
(Genesis 1:3)

Then the Lord stretched out His hand and touched my mouth, and the
Lord said to me, "Behold, I have put My words in your mouth.
"See, I have appointed you this day over the nations and over the
kingdoms, To pluck up and to break down,
To destroy and to overthrow, To build and to plant."
(Jeremiah 1:9-10)

Why did God give Jeremiah authority?

_____

_____

_____

_____

_____

A prophet is not only to repeat what God is saying, a prophet declares things into being by the "Word of the Lord."

Surely the Lord God does nothing
Unless He reveals His secret counsel
To His servants the prophets.
(Amos 3:7)

The Power of Declaration

_____

_____

_____

_____

_____

The hand of the Lord was upon me, and He brought me out by the Spirit of the Lord and set me down in the middle of the valley; and it was full of bones. He caused me to pass among them round about, and behold, there were very many on the surface of the valley; and lo, they were very dry. He said to me, "Son of man, can these bones live?" And I answered, "O Lord God, You know." Again He said to me, "Prophesy over these bones and say to them, 'O dry bones, hear the word of the Lord.' Thus says the Lord God to these bones, 'Behold, I will cause breath to enter you that you may come to life. I will put sinews on you, make flesh grow back on you, cover you with skin and put breath in you that you may come alive; and you will know that I am the Lord. '" So I prophesied as I was commanded; and as I prophesied, there was a noise, and behold, a rattling; and the bones came together, bone to its bone. And I looked, and behold, sinews were on them, and flesh grew and skin covered them; but there was no breath in them. Then He said to me, "Prophesy to the breath, prophesy, son of man, and say to the breath, 'Thus says the Lord God, "Come from the four winds, O breath, and breathe on these slain, that they come to life."' So I prophesied as He commanded me, and the breath came into them, and they came to life and stood on their feet, an exceedingly great army. (Ezekiel 37:1-10)

• God created the world by _____ it into existence.

• We have the same potential when we _____ the Word of the Lord.

• Prophecy is _____ speaking through a person.

• Declaration _____ world events and history.

PART 3

A HEALTHY PROPHETIC COMMUNITY

A HEALTHY PROPHETIC COMMUNITY

INTRODUCTION

A safe and stable community is vital if we are going to seek the gift of prophecy. There is a great deal of trouble in relation to this gift; there always has been. Prophecy is like fire - powerful, useful, yet also dangerous. We must create some boundaries to protect us all from getting 'burned.' I have realized that the success of a prophetic culture is anchored in healthy relationships. The number one relationship that must be tight is between the prophetic ministry and the senior leader. When a prophetic community honors the leadership structure, there is safety and unity in the house. We also honor one another, confronting in love and always encouraging one another, believing the best about each other. This will create a spiritual greenhouse that allows people to grow stronger and faster.

_____

_____

_____

_____

_____

But now in Christ Jesus you who formerly were far off have been brought near by the blood of Christ. For He Himself is our peace, who made both groups into one and broke down the barrier of the dividing wall, by abolishing in His flesh the enmity, which is the Law of commandments contained in ordinances, so that in Himself He might make the two into one new man, thus establishing peace, and might reconcile them both in one body to God through the cross, by it having put to death the enmity. And He came and preached peace to you who were far away, and peace to those who were near; for through Him we both have our access in one Spirit to the Father. So then you are no longer strangers and aliens, but you are fellow citizens with the saints, and are of God's household, having been built on the foundation of the apostles and prophets, Christ Jesus Himself being the corner stone, in whom the whole building, being fitted together, is growing into a holy temple in the Lord, (Ephesians 2:13-21)

1. False Prophets

Jesus warns us about false prophets. He said, "Beware of the false prophets, who come to you in sheep's clothing, but inwardly are ravenous wolves. You will know them by their fruits *(Matthew 7:15-16)*. They will even be able to walk in signs and wonders. How will we be able to recognize them? Jesus said that we would recognize them by their fruits. Fruit is different than gifting. Fruit points to the character of a person, not their ability or personality. Fruit is most often revealed in the context of relationships.

- They continually speak of things that you don't understand *(Not the goal of prophecy)*
- They seem more spiritual than Jesus, and more spiritual than the leadership *(self-righteous)*
- They expose people's shortcomings *(not love)*
- They flatter you to lure you in *(control, manipulation)*
- They seem to know everything but profess humility *(lack of humility)*
- They say all the time, "The Lord told me..." *(Not open to input)*
- They "love" the leadership but... "the leadership doesn't get it" *(dishonor)*
- They lead people to depend on them *(co-dependent, insecure)*
- They don't have fathers *(wounded, independent)*
- They are not open to correction *(isolated, unwise)*
- They have followers but no leaders *(no one is good enough to lead them)*
- They make you feel as though you need to catch up *(opposite of encouragement)*
- They blame every negative word against them on spiritual warfare *(foolish)*
- They blame every problem in their life on the devil *(lack of taking responsibility)*
- They love to tell you all the stuff they have heard and seen *(boastful)*

What is so luring about a false prophet?

_____

_____

_____

_____

*Let no one keep defrauding you of your prize by delighting in self-abasement
and the worship of the angels, taking his stand on visions he has seen,
inflated without cause by his fleshly mind. (Colossians 2:18)*

We are from God; he who knows God listens to us; he who is not from God does not listen to us. By this we know the spirit of truth and the spirit of error. (1 John 4:6)

Obey your leaders and submit to them, for they keep watch over your souls as those who will give an account. Let them do this with joy and not with grief, for this would be unprofitable for you. (Hebrews 13:17)

How does honor for leadership protect people?

_____

_____

_____

_____

2. Judging Prophetic Words

Paul tells us to judge the prophetic words that are spoken. This may seem scary for the one giving the word, but as our minds are renewed it will actually be a comfort. We all have the potential to be 'off.' I don't know about you but if I'm off base I would like to know! I would hope someone would tell me. We have to get used to our words being evaluated and also evaluate the words given to us. This keeps us all accountable and creates a safe place to experiment without the danger of becoming a false prophet. Consider it like a referee in a soccer game. We all want a good game and the referee makes sure that everyone is playing by the rules.

Questions to evaluate a prophetic word

1. Was the person's attitude and underlying spirit humble?
2. How was the method of delivery?
3. Did the word go through the proper channels?
4. Is this person a part of a healthy family of believers?
5. Is this person submitted to authority?
6. Did the word contradict scripture?
7. Was it a confirmation or out of left field?
8. Did I feel the presence of God when I heard it?
9. What do my closest friends think about the word?
10. Was it edifying?

Let two or three prophets speak, and let the others pass judgment.
(1 Corinthians 14:29)

- We judge prophecy because it is best done in _____.

- We judge prophecy because we want _____.

- We judge prophecy because the prophecy is not an exact _____.

_____

_____

_____

*For you can all prophesy one by one, so that all may learn and all may be
exhorted; and the spirits of prophets are subject to prophets; for God is not a
God of confusion but of peace, as in all the churches of the saints.*
(1 Corinthians 14:31-33)

3. Seeing People the Way God Sees Them

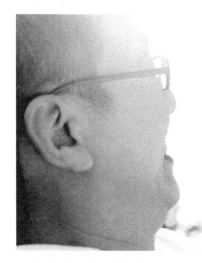

A significant part of prophecy addresses identity. God uses the gift to tell people who He has made them to be. Prophecy will connect a group by helping them to see each other as God sees them. This transforms the person receiving the word but also changes everyone's perspective about the person receiving ministry. The gift of prophecy calls people into their true identity: it is not designed to reveal what people have done wrong.

- Celebrate who people _____ without stumbling over who they're _____.

- You are speaking to _____ not sinners.

- Believers are prone to _____.

- When you misdiagnose, you _____.

- Trust that the people have a _____ with God.

But you are a chosen race, a royal priesthood, a holy nation, a people for God's own possession, so that you may proclaim the excellencies of Him who has called you out of darkness into His marvelous light; for you once were not a people, but now you are the people of God; you had not received mercy, but now you have received mercy.
(1 Peter 2:9-10)

4. How the Prophetic Partners with the Rest of the Body

God the Father in His wisdom set up the leadership structure of the church. He made Jesus the Head of the church, then the 5-Fold ministry (Apostles, Prophets, Pastors, Teachers and Evangelists), then Elders and Deacons. Some have had a problem with these positions, however, we cannot take the liberty to change what God has established because of our personal feelings. There have been those who have abused authority but we must reestablish the Biblical structure that God has set up. When we in humility honor our leaders, we honor God who put our leaders in place. Prophecy is one piece of the puzzle in the overall structure of the Body of Christ.

Having been built on the foundation of the apostles and prophets, Christ Jesus Himself being the corner stone. (Ephesians 2:20)

There is one body and one Spirit, just as also you were called in one hope of your calling; one Lord, one faith, one baptism, one God and Father of all who is over all and through all and in all. But to each one of us grace was given according to the measure of Christ's gift. Therefore it says, "When HE ascended on high, HE led captive A host of captives, And HE gave gifts to men."
… And He gave some as apostles, and some as prophets, and some as evangelists, and some as pastors and teachers, for the equipping of the saints for the work of service, to the building up of the body of Christ; until we all attain to the unity of the faith, and of the knowledge of the Son of God, to a mature man, to the measure of the stature which belongs to the fullness of Christ. (Ephesians 4:4-13)

God the Father in His wisdom set up the leadership structure of the church.

How does the prophetic enhance the rest of the Body?

_____

_____

_____

_____

- The Church is God's instrument to bring _____ to earth.

- Jesus is the Head and _____ of the Church.

- Jesus set up the five-fold ministry to _____ the Church.

- The prophetic gift _____ to its' part in the overall structure God set up.

- The prophet is seeing only _____ part of the overall picture.

- The prophetic ministry is to _____ the Lord and interpret what God is doing and when.

- The prophetic ministry is to provide _____ to the Body.

- The prophetic ministry is to establish _____ between the members of the Body and God.

Now at this time some prophets came down from Jerusalem to Antioch. One of them named Agabus stood up and began to indicate by the Spirit that there would certainly be a great famine all over the world. And this took place in the reign of Claudius. And in the proportion that any of the disciples had means, each of them determined to send a contribution for the relief of the brethren living in Judea. And this they did, sending it in charge of Barnabas and Saul to the elders. (Acts 11:27-30)

Judas and Silas, also being prophets themselves, encouraged and strengthened the brethren with a lengthy message. (Acts 15:32)

5. Identity Before Gifting

The gifts are not God's reward for good behavior. In other words, people that are highly gifted are not more favored. Gifting can be deceiving in the sense that it can mislead a person to think that they are close with God because they are flowing in the gifts of the Spirit. We see this in Matthew chapter seven when Jesus said, "Many will say to Me on that day, 'Lord, Lord, did we not prophesy in Your name, and in Your name cast out demons, and in Your name perform many miracles?' And then I will declare to them, 'I never knew you; depart from ME, you who practice lawlessness *(Matthew 7:22-23)*. Ouch! Our character and personal relationship with God are way more important than being 'gifted'

49

or dynamic. Our identity as a child of God is not rooted in what we do but in who we are. When people have an identity deficit, they are often drawn to the gifts to receive praise and feel important. We are to desire the gifts but be enamored by the identity that we have through the cross.

> *The seventy returned with joy, saying, "Lord, even the demons are subject to us in Your name." And He said to them, "I was watching Satan fall from heaven like lightning. Behold, I have given you authority to tread on serpents and scorpions, and over all the power of the enemy, and nothing will injure you. Nevertheless do not rejoice in this, that the spirits are subject to you, but rejoice that your names are recorded in heaven." (Luke 10:17-20)*

_____

_____

_____

- Our _____ with God is more important than our _____ to God.

- Our maturity level is revealed by _____, not gifts.

- Our gifts do not determine our _____.

- To seek the gifts for praise reveals a _____ in our _____ as a child of God.

- We _____ people because of who they are, not what they do.

When God uses you, praise Him for how good He is!

6. Core Beliefs

When we hear a sermon or read our Bible, we will each interpret it differently than those around us. We all see the world through tinted glasses because we have a set of core beliefs that were developed by our unique experiences. Core beliefs are the very essence of how we see ourselves, other people, the world, and the future. Sometimes, these core beliefs become 'activated' in certain situations. Teaching, events and people all shaped your belief system to what it is today. These beliefs may not always be at the surface but they influence your thinking and decision making. A good set of core beliefs can bring about good fruit in a person's life. On the other hand, poor beliefs can taint everything you perceive and release. The way you hear God and prophesy often reveals your core belief system. The goal is to align your beliefs with the Word of God so that we will see Him purely and minister from a healthy place.

Examples of Core Beliefs:

- Nothing is free in this world.
- I am unlovable.
- If you want something done, do it yourself.
- People are stupid.
- Don't show weakness.
- An expensive car means that someone is successful.
- When people praise me, I am valuable.
- I am not good enough.
- Leaders are all…

Kingdom Core Beliefs

- Everything is possible with God.
- There is always a solution.
- Every person was made by God for great things.
- There is hope in every circumstance.
- Leaders are positioned to help me becom e successful.
- I know God will provide for me.
- I am powerful in Christ.

> *"While you have the Light, believe in the Light, so that you
> may become sons of Light." (John 12:36)*

7. Changing Your World

The final chapter in this class is focused on taking what you have learned and applying it in the secular environment. Joseph was able to interpret Pharaoh's dream and eventually became second in command in all of Egypt. The gift of prophecy must work at the supermarket, at your workplace and in your neighborhood. The Holy Spirit desires to speak to non-Christians and wants to use you. The main goal of the prophetic is to reconcile people to the Father. We are responsible to change our atmosphere and set people free wherever we are by the power of prophecy!

Prophecy Protocol

• Treat people with _____.

• Use _____ language.

• _____ does not make prophecy more powerful.

• Be _____. You release what you feel inside.

• Pay attention to what the _____ is doing.

• Be friendly and _____ conversations wherever you are.

Your Testimony is Prophecy

The testimony of Jesus is the spirit of prophecy.
(Revelation 19:10)

Everyone has a testimony. Everyone has a story to share about how Jesus rescued them. Testify that you are saved. Your knees may be knocking but when you begin telling your testimony, you will enter into the spirit of prophecy. Before you know it, the Spirit will be talking through you.

What is your testimony?

_____

_____

_____

_____

_____

_____

_____

_____

_____

_____

_____

_____
_____
_____
_____
_____
_____
_____
_____
_____
_____
_____
_____
_____
_____
_____
_____

*But if all prophesy, and an unbeliever or an ungifted man enters, he is
convicted by all, he is called to account by all; the secrets of his heart
are disclosed; and so he will fall on his face and worship God, declaring
that God is certainly among you. (1 Corinthians 14:24-25)*

*"Ask of Me, and I will surely give the nations as Your inheritance,
And the very ends of the earth as Your possession." (Psalms 2:8)*

NOTES

Made in the USA
Monee, IL
26 September 2022

14539286R10033